# BROKEN LITTLE PIECES

## New Tales from The Baron

# BILLY J. BARNUM

ISBN 979-8-218-37505-8 (Paperback)

ISBN 9798224747573 (Digital)

Author signature page

# Elephant in the Room

Words unspoken

Spirit broken

It will get to you

Man I'm not joking


Vaulted ceilings

Way up high

Fifteen hundred square feet

And all you want to do is cry


Lots of air

But hard to breathe

It's invisible

And it won't leave


Unbroken stares

It needs to be addressed soon

It fills all spaces

The elephant in the room

# Dropping Pennies

There's a man that likes to drop pennies

He drops them everywhere

In a shopping center parking lot

He drops them without care


There's a guy on the corner

With a sign that reads "will work for food"

But the man still drops his pennies

Whenever he's in the mood


He drops them here

He drops them there

Sometimes he drops them

Everywhere


Find a penny, pick it up

If the head is looking at you

All day long

You'll have good luck


Maybe someday

He'll start dropping quarters

Or maybe someday

He'll even drop water

Continued... ➡

For people that have none

As they pray to the sky

He may just show up

And be the water guy


As they drink up their thirst

'Till it's quenched and all done

And they all shake his hand

As they bask in the sun

# Broken Little Pieces

Broken little pieces

Lying shattered on the ground

If the pieces are still big enough

They can go another round


But this time the pieces were too small

Just millions upon millions of shards

As the dealer exclaimed "no more bets"

We just pushed them aside then folded our cards


Imagine your whole house is on fire

And all you have is a small fire extinguisher

And the truck arrives ten minutes too late

Speechless and out of breath, no words to use to tell her


To stare at the char

Would never do good

It's time to move on

Some call me strong, some misunderstood


Broken little pieces

Nothing left so don't look back

Pull up your pants and be a big boy now

And stop slipping through the cracks

# More, More, More

You always gave me extra time
You always gave me extra space
When I fell down, you'd pick me up
I never fell from grace

I always felt that I belonged
I always felt that I fit in
There were some times when I would lose
But I'd usually mostly win

Never fearing needing more
Never asked cause I was given
Count the night sky lucky stars
Love the life I'm living

One day Jupiter fell out of line
One day it had to find me
Now all the space, and all that time
Crushed inside and blind me

Spiraling out of control now
Spiraling now don't pity the poor
Don't be a glutton and squander your riches
Don't be ungrateful wanting more, more, more

# More, More, More

You always gave me extra time.

You always gave me extra space

When I fell down, you'd pick me up

I never fell from grace

I always fe...

I always fe...

There wel...

But I'd da...

Never lear...

Never ask...

Count the...

Love the li...

One day I...

One day it had to find me

Crushed inside and blind me

Spinning out of control now

# The Ghost Inside Me (Part 2)

Oh! my word
He's back again
Putting words in my mind
And controlling my hand

This time I see visions
Of magical worlds
And fantastical creatures
One by one they unfurl

And they lay out a landscape
Of wondrous hues
While my hand keeps on scribbling
I'm enjoying the view

Everyone's laughing
Except one has a frown
As I ask "what's the matter?"
Hangs his head to the ground

He says "just you keep on writing"
And I'll be happy soon
As a glow comes over the ocean
From the light of the moon

Continued...➡

He says I shall not leave you

We have many more books to complete

But when it's time for you to join me

It will be my honor for us to meet

# Mandatory Must

Contrails blowing sideways
As they wafted in the wind
You reneged your hand in spades
 Now they want you to rescind

Then they strapped you to the wing
Crazy is as crazy does
One small slip and you are done
All the bees they love to buzz

Just imagine simple times
Climb aboard and cast your net
Then the prize eludes the soul
man, you ain't seen nothing yet

In this quirky quacky life
In the stands you're yelling "peanuts!"
All your friends at karaoke
Are out there screaming "man is he nuts!"

As we wrap up this affair
Singing *"Another one bites the dust"*
Imagination will prevail
It's a mandatory must

# Leaving

The rocket's leaving so hurry up

Put on your helmet and climb aboard

If you don't hurry, you're gonna miss it

You'll never get to leave this world


And then the countdown now begins

Flames start shooting all around

Houston, we have liftoff

As we push away from the ground


The higher and higher we go

Leaves me wondering why I'm leaving

Simple little solvable problems

My mind retreats to unbelieving


And why I had to go away

Instead of stand and face the truth

If Watson had to solve this puzzle

His response would have been "cannot compute"


If I ever make it back to earth

I promise that I'll try

A little harder every day

To find the answer to the why's

# Ink on That Paper

You were going nowhere
Until you put the pen on to the page
And then you sang a three-part harmony
There you were up on that stage

The words came alive
All the jugglers and the clowns
And the man on the tightrope
Saying he will not come down

Cause the pages they lifted him
So, so high off the ground
Then he became the ringmaster
With no sad thoughts and no need for a frown

So, he decided to hit the road
His sack tied to a stick
And his whistle was contagious
As they watch his feet a skip

Bright eyed and brand new
Because the pages are not blank
Put that ink on that paper
Then it's you you'll have to thank

# Butterflies

When's the last time

That butterflies flew from your soul?

And you had that nervous feeling

Like a child playing in the snow


Feeling cautious and scared

But still following it forward

And your lips would not move

None escape, you have no words


Then your thumbs start to fidget

And your knees start to shake

And your heart is beating so hard

It seems way too much to take


Then you find words, but start to stutter

A little drool I guess won't hurt

Then she stares into your eyes

and says "I'm a little flirt"


Pretty soon you'll need a defibrillator

Just to stay up on your feet

Palms are sweaty and getting worse

You'll have to get something to eat

Continued...➡

But stay away from sugar

Cause she'll cause cavities

And if you get a sweet tooth

She'll bring you to your knees

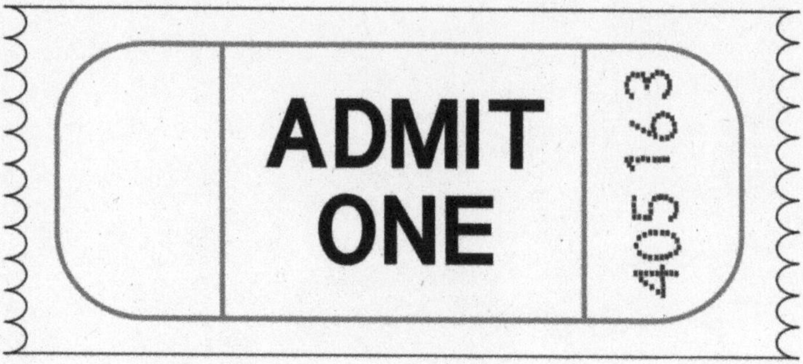
ADMIT
ONE
405163

# Captivation

Like the beginning of a movie
and you just want to see more
Cause the intro got you so hooked
On to the carpet and in through the door

And the epic music winds you up
Now you're waiting for the next scene
As the monster now enters the room
Hands over your mouth you start to scream

And so the story carries on
In the horse drawn carriage
You're along for the ride
Popcorn for the marriage

Intermission, don't you dare!
You'll see me turn into a beast
Just ask me where the sun will rise
It will be always be in the east

We've come down to the final scene
As you bid farewell, so long my friend
You should have known right from the start
That this would have to end

# Worth its Weight in Gold

You stepped into a brand-new world
And shortly after things turned sour
Your head was floating way up high
As you got high on the power

But keep in mind there's always someone higher
That will put you back where you belong
And when you're singing way out loud
Nobody will be singing along

They will call you silent Sally
The dominos stood tall but now have fallen
The valley of the pines
Can you hear the voices calling?

They call to you to bring you home
Who's the big man now?
All possessions stripped and gone
A stoned-faced look of wow!

Lessons learned and stories listened
Stranger than fiction so you're told
It all comes back you can be sure
It's worth its weight in gold

# Worth Its Weight in Gold

Your head was floating way up high
As you got high on the power

But keep in mind there's always someone higher
Nobody will be singing...

The dominos stood tall but now have fallen,
The valley of the pines
Can you hear the voices calling?

They call to you to bring you home
Who's the big man now?
All possessions stripped and gone
A stoned-faced look of wow!

Lessons learned and stories listened
Stranger than fiction so you're told
It all comes back you can be sure
It's worth its weight in gold

# Ride the Rapids

I rode the rapids
And prayed just to stay in the boat
If I hit a rock and flew out
I wondered how well I would float

But nothing ventured, nothing gained
I took my chance and paddled
And sank that oar and pushed through
The war's not won, let's take the battle

Baby steps it's getting deeper
Placid water has finally called
And just ahead now in my sight
One hundred and fifty feet falls

As panic sets in I must stay calm
A life full of memories flashes by
As the wisdom of words, I hear an echo
Then I leave the boat and start to fly

She says "I told you I'd never leave you
And I'd always protect my baby girl"
If you can't see it doesn't mean it's not there
A chance to deserve to be in this world

# Inspiration

I didn't know I needed it

This to you I swear

As I turned the page between my fingers

Running down my cheek, a solitary tear


Oh! My God! The words they moved me

What the hell am I reading?

A poets pain

And I can feel his heart break bleeding


Conveying words

Oh my! how he conveyed

As he smashed his guitar

And he exits the stage


The fire was lit

And my fingers were burned

Then I picked up my pen

As I dreamed and I yearned


Knowing something was coming

But not knowing what

The emotions they stirred

All the feels in my gut

Continued.. ➡

Like a splash on the canvas

Painting words, keeping time

Hear the second-hand ticking

Creating beautiful rhymes


And it comes out of nowhere

Brings you joy, brings you Zen

'Till the ink runneth dry

As I resteth my pen

# Stone of Destiny

With hyperbolic speeding sound

She left without a curse

With future's uncertain and can't be found

She hid it in her purse


And no one checked or even looked

Like a flash she was gone

The stone of destiny has now been hidden

Just how now shall we carry on?


It loses power without the scepter

Everyday it's gone humanity gets bleaker

To rely on the stone for so many years

Without it we all grow weaker


What if collectively we all pray

And say, "my God now can you hear me?"

He answers back "I hear you my children

Acknowledge now that you fear me"


We all nod yes and every ruin

It's all brand new and disappears

Some things are more powerful than a stone

Just bow your head and say your prayers

# Tall Fishing Tale

I sat at the dock

And baited my hook

As a seal swam by

I took one more look


Then I pulled back my rod

And let the line go

Turned the radio up

And sipped my drink real slow


It's a tug on the line

As my bobber went under

Then I reached for my rod

And started reeling fast as thunder


The waves in the water

Were getting closer and closer

What's almost in front of me?

Imagination's taking over


Then I saw a large tail

As it leapt off the hook

It was truly fantastic

As I only read it in books

Continued.. ➡

A beautiful mermaid
She swam up to the dock
My face stunned in awe
Like cement out of shock

She said "now that you've found me
I'll always be here"
If you ever need to talk
I'll lend you my ear

As my face was unfrozen
And my vision turned clear
With a blink of an eye
She was gone, disappeared

I never told anyone
They'd call it a tall fishing tale
But I go back there from time to time
To cast my line and exhale

# Spin the Wheel

Step right up and spin the wheel

And I'll control your fate

You paid in blood to get this far

And now it's much too late


Round and round so many choices

Anywhere it can stop

You gulp your throat as the wheel slows

And to your knees then you drop


It stopped at "spare his life"

Release those chains and set him free!

No more punishment shall be given

Guards just leave him be


As they drive you far from misery

And release you far from nowhere

The little things in life

Somehow no more you shall care


Things that once annoyed

A poof and they are gone

A single prayer you say out loud

A wish to carry on

Continued... ➡

And to grow old and pass this along
To anyone who listens
Oh! See the sky it shines so bright
As I squint from all its glisten

And there's a sparkle in my eye
For every new beginning
There is no loss, it's far behind
As the wheel keeps on spinning

# Always There

In the times you needed me the most
You thought I wasn't there
In those times you felt so helpless
You thought I didn't care

You thought "How could you abandon me?"
When I needed lifting up
You looked around to see me
Not in sight, and not enough

Then he said "I was there for all of those times"
The troubled and the bad
And every tear you've shed in life
From the happy to the sad

Those times that you felt weak
I would not let you fall
I held you up and you always thanked me
As you smiled and you paused

Because you didn't see me
Doesn't mean I wasn't there
Trust me my child ...
I was always there

In the times you needed me the most

You thought I wasn't there

You thought I...

When I need...

You looked a...

Not in sight...

Then he said...

From the hap...

Those times that you felt weak

I would not let you fall

I held you up and you always thanked me

As you smiled and you paused.

Because you didn't see me

Doesn't mean I wasn't there

Trust me my child...

I was always there

# Don't You Dare

Don't you dare tell me I don't want it

Don't you dare tell me I don't need it

Don't you dare tell me, just don't!

It's my dream and dammit I'll feed it


Don't you dare push me away

Don't you dare look as you shun me

I've worked for this way too long

And trust me my desire is still hungry


Don't you dare tell me I can't

Don't you dare tell me I won't

I'll be flying so high, blinding light in the sky

As I return to earth a lightning bolt


Don't you dare tell me you're sorry

Don't you dare tell me, just don't!

Of all the things that you have done to me

This one has hurt me the most

# Wasting Time

You say "I'll do it tomorrow"

Then the next day, then the next

Today is not a good day

Maybe tomorrow will be the best


But one day it just hit you

"What if tomorrow never comes?"

"Is my last breath in ten minutes?"

And I never get it done


So you put everything down

And changed your social plans

And said "If I don't stick to my word"

How will they measure me as a man?


They'd say "he'd always say he'd do it"

But sadly never got it done

He thought time would last forever

Until time ran out and there was none


I hope that in his next life

He applies this life's lessons learned

When the candle burns at both ends

Sometimes you might get burned

# Starfish on The Beach

A pocket full of daffodils

Like starfish on the beach

In light year travels seems so far

A tortured soul just out of reach


You jump right in, a shark attack

You punch him in the eye

The bird it comes and picks you up

Suddenly, you're in the sky


As they sing bye bye birdie

You wave and hear the cheers

A mother bows her head

A tragedy of what's down there


Keep your eye on the puzzle

Somehow eludes, the final piece

You'll search for it a lifetime

Like the starfish on the beach

# While We All Burn

The sky is burning

The earth is yearning

For relief

The human thief


They live their lives in numbers

While we're all going under

They said one hundred years

A few years later now everyone cares


It's always been broadcast

For so many years that've passed

They kept on lining their pockets

While our eyes bulge out of our sockets


The trees are on fire

Lightning strikes and transpires

Just why they didn't stop

Greedy people grew the crops


Just huddle in your bubble

'til it pops then we're in trouble

If we're so smart, why won't we learn?

Scorching sun while we all burn

# Rambles

Crumpets and tea crumbs

This noise hurts my ear drums

What you call is magic

Appears something tragic


There's a mist on the wall

Refusing to fall

Forming clouds in my eyes

Making looks of surprise


Hey man! Pass the baton

So we all can move on

The ribbon's been cut

And the fish lost his guts


Gather 'round for the feast

My invitation to say the least

And by now what the hell

Timmy fell down in the well


All these rambles in shambles

While the Texan he gambles

Then the deuce turns to queen

If you know what I mean

# Gaze Upon a Night Sky

I gaze upon a night sky

That shall never last 'til day

The trajectory orbit we once knew

Time would not let stay


With champagne wishes and caviar dreams

Remembering how we drew pictures from stars

Then we'd see a miracle one shooting

Lying up on the roofs, on our backs, on our cars


To infinity and beyond

Put our hopes in a basket

Never thinking that soon

That we'd build our own caskets


One fell swoop living woken up nightmares

As we all turn white as ghosts

Somebody threw a nuclear party

And we all ended up as its hosts


As we all heard the bang

We recalled when they'd say

And we'd gaze upon a night sky

That never lasted 'til day

# Gaze Upon a Night Sky

I gaze upon a night sky

That shall never last, til day

The trajectory orbit we once knew

With champagne w...

Remembering how...

Lying up on the roo...

To infinity and bey...

Put our hopes in a...

And we all ended up as its hosts

We recalled when they'd say

And we'd gaze upon a night sky

That never lasted til day

# The Island is Burning

The island is burning

And there's nowhere to go

Except jump in the ocean

And they didn't go slow


All the boats were burned too

Could not sail away

Just an ocean to jump in

Ashes of memories, what a horrible day


A quadrillion gallons around them

No sprinkler system in place

A mass of land in the middle of

Gods glorious saving grace


They say tears from the sun

Lit that island on fire

It's a story from elders

That made the tales grow higher


They bulldozed it all down

Rebuilt it shiny and new

As they evolved and they learned

Humans new golden rule

# In the Fire Light Glow

we stacked the wood and lit a match
and it started off real slow
we heard the crackle and I seen the shine
of your face in the fire light glow

mysteriously unfamiliar
but eerily familiar just as well
as the glow grew brighter and brighter
right then I could tell

that's a face even without the glow
I could love for life
To thee I wed etcetera, etcetera
The bride all dressed in white

God was riding the train
Thirty-five feet from the gown
As the pedestal lifted you high
He says go now and don't let me down

And just to think
On that one chilly night
We lit a spark
And all the passions ignite

Continued.. ➡

That smoldering fire

And even we didn't know

What would turn into this

By the fire light glow

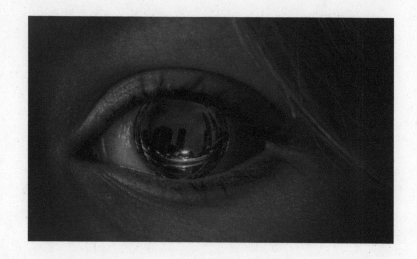

# Searching for a cause

He said nothing can stop you

Once you get inspiration

Where you're trying to sail

It will be your destination


Just plant your flag

And call it yours

Keep rowing that boat

With your magical oars


It's like lightning it struck

And a light bulb went off

And before it happened

You were searching for a cause


You heard it, you read it

You watched it live

Then a feeling took over

It all started to jive


You're a standout among peers

You're the toast of the nation

When you get it you'll know

Follow it intently, be the next inspiration

# On to the next

If you've struggled to pay the rent

And somehow made it through

On to the next

Take a breath


If you've had a loved one in the hospital

And they came home and healed

On to the next

Take a breath


If you've had a loved one in a war

And now they're right beside you

On to the next

Take a breath


If you've had a child born premature

And now they're bigger than you

On to the next

Take a breath


If you've dreamt something

And all your dreams have come true

On to the next

Take a breath

Continued... ➡

If you've prayed that you get to do

On to the next

Well then … on to the next

Take a breath

# The Magician

The magician works his magic

But the illusion's never clear

He takes his wand and taps his hat

And then he disappears


Not quite knowing where he went

Curiosity fills your mind

Will you accept that he is gone?

Or will you search to find


The answer or the man

It's a complicated equation

Like doing trigonometry

How the grape became the raisin


The waiter yells out "dinner!"

As we all put on our bibs

A perfect feast for all to find

We soon will call our dibs


Imagine that not knowing

Can be very beneficial

As we live our lives in wonder

Never worrying about the issues

Continued.. ➡

That consume us everyday

Some are large, and some are small

Some we miss

And some we heed the call


But the ones of most importance

You can bet that we'll take care of

As we pass around the bread

The magician reappears releasing a white dove

# Snowed In

Winter's getting colder

Like it's never been before

The avalanche is coming

The snow is piling at my door


I'm running out of rations

Wood is low, so much for heat

And I'm not sure just how long I'll last

It's the nature of the beast


So I decide to write awhile

Hoping someone reads my work

When I am gone all that remains

Will be the pecking of the birds


And they will fly and carry me

To my final destination

Maybe I'll come back as a tree

To rest at my final station

# The Journey

Once there was a man

Who wrote magical words on parchment paper

Imagination steamed out from his mind

In a mystical invisible vapor


His words transformed his readers

From a pauper to a prince

From a king into a common

With the princess they did dance


Those who couldn't walk

Were now able to fly

And those who couldn't talk

Spoke in paragraphs with their eyes


And for those that felt so helpless

They now had valiant hope

They would reach another rung

Just before the end of their rope


The blind that couldn't see

Read in braille and they could see now

And for those that couldn't hear

Heard the trumpets blaring out loud

Continued... ➡

The man he didn't know

That his words held so much power

And he almost stopped his writings

Just before the final hour


Now with testimonies clear

All the noise be gone the rage

He continues on his journey

And lays his words upon the page

# Unfinished

I'm an unfinished poem

With unfinished rhymes

I feel lonely but hopeful

In these unfinished times


I have unfinished business

And unfinished plans

For I am only human

I'm an unfinished man


Will the poem be finished

When fate beckons its call?

With so many things unfinished

And so little time to finish it all


I guess that's the puzzle

With the unfinished pieces

And all we have left

In an unfinished thesis


But this poem won't go out

Without giving it a try

With one last finished effort

And the wink of the eye

# No Dry Eye

You cannot stop the unforeseen
You cannot stop just where you've been
But you can change where you will go
Your destiny will make you grow

So big and tall with food for thought
Our past battles won that our fathers have fought
With perpetual grace we always march on
To leave a beautiful world for our daughters and sons

We march to a beat of a different drum
Then we break out our guitars and we start to strum
We'll create an enchanting and catchy tune
By the time we are done you'll soon start to swoon

And the world will rejoice with unfathomable glee
As the masses all gather and then drop to their knees
Then they'll raise up their hands palms facing the sky
As the waterworks begin leaving not one dry eye

# Black Rose 2

I have returned

To plant the seed

The world has learned

To stop its greed


The moon so bright

And whole again

Like you told me father

I'd know just when


Now dig a hole

And bring me rain

So this thirsty seed

Can breathe again


This little sprout

Will grow so tall

Through its towering journey

It will create it all


And black as night

Just like it was

And give it light

And give it love

Continued... ➡

There'll be new tales to tell
About the thorn
Gone away be the past
Of how it was scorned

And a new light will shine
And a new day will come
And the children will sing
As the crying was done

The rose has the power
We are healed leave us be
As we focus on the future
Making new memories

# Unthinkable

You lick your fingers to fix her hair

Then send her off to school

Innocence in all its rarity

To learn the golden rules


Never knowing that a monster

Has awoken and breathing fire

You never thought you'd get that call

That would turn you into a crier


But that day it came

It was on the news

Everyone was watching

And they were looking at you


As the newsman asks questions

The camera pans to your face

As you stare in disgust

From the tragedy that just took place


The cop says "If we gave you 5 minutes alone with him"

What would you do?

As your inner demon seeps out

You say "I would break every rule"

Continued... ➡

I would rip off his face
And feed it to his dog
I would commit unspeakable acts
Are you following along?

Then you come back to your senses
And say "I would pray for his soul"
Because where he is heading
I guess God only knows

# Chains

The chains that hold me

They cannot bind

No matter how tight

This creative free mind


It bunches and tangles

As it tries to restrain

All the wonderful words

That are contained in this brain


They will splash on the page

Making colors so bright

And shine like a moonbeam

On the darkest of nights


I yell "Hey holder of the key!"

Are you really even there?

As you pull tighter and tighter

Like you don't even care


These chains won't define me

As I finally break free

To create such strong chains

You must be cowardly and weak

# Mega Storm

While you were sleeping

The world just fell apart

The winds they came and destroyed our homes

And someone called it art


They put it in a million pictures

And sold it to the news

As we sat there cold and homeless

Surely, we must not share the same views


As we scrounge to get a bite to eat

You're at dinner eating steak

As we stare out at the rubble

A little more our hearts will break


Well thank God we're still alive

And the news says thank God too

As they finally setup a hotline

While they're traveling on their cruise


They check in from time to time

To make a little extra cash

Then they realize they can only milk this cow so long

Then they leave us in the past

Continued... ➡

No more how've you been

We're now part of the norm

As they sit and await destruction

From the next mega storm

# Unhindering Ghouls

Chairs and tables

In vacancy

I enter in

Just let me be


Clocks tell time

I think they do

As a chair is filled

In clear plain view


Nothing beats

The importance of the man

As the train chugs on

I think I can, I think I can


As day light fades

I take my cue

I'm lost in space

On a ship of fools


You tip the waiter

Should I tip too?

It's all been odd

Unhindering ghouls

# A Dying Star

It has so many stages
Before it dies into the night
So many have wished upon it
Before it had its final plight

It flickered and it gleamed
For a hundred thousand years
And for those that gazed upon it
Through the laughter and the tears

The world has changed a lot
But the star has stayed the same
Its coordinates firmly locked
As many have given it a name

Something special to them
But to the star just ordinary
Just plain old Mr. Bright Light
Not even close, but quite contrary

As it sputtered, then it winked
Then its sparkle became extinguished
As I gazed upon the void
From a light that's now relinquished

# The Good Ones Always Go Too Soon

When you take your final curtain

And you take your final bow

People that haven't heard yet

Will still be saying "I wonder what he's doing now?"


Not knowing that you're even gone

But still curious about your life

Reaching out to you where you are

Makes your spirit dance and glide


Because you made an impact

Lasting far beyond your years

And yes, it really matters

feeling that somebody cares


if you live with honesty and integrity

and treat your friends with respect

to be remembered long after you're gone

is what you should expect


they'll say "the good ones always go too soon"

and they always go too fast

but they sure made a lot of memories

for a long time, they will last

# Scars

My scars they don't define me

They're just memories of the past

And every time I look at them

There are many questions to ask


Each one has its own place

It stays right where it belongs

It reminds me of the right way

And reminds me of the wrongs


The scars that are visible

Are the ones upon my skin

But the most pain that I feel

Are from the ones that lie within


You see those ones never really heal

They just dissipate with time

And the thing I love the most

Is that these scars are all mine


I know you can relate

Because you must have scars too

And you'll carry on just like me

And know just what to do

# Silence

And in the sound of silence

I can hear my thoughts out loud

And even though I'm all alone

It feels like I'm in a crowd


I hear it echo back

As I begin my famous speech

The reverb is so loud

So bad that silence seems out of reach


I take the podium, as I begin

I ramble off the intro

The crowd reacts with cheers

If they only knew what I know


I'm in my mind not really there

But they still cheer loud as can be

As I stop talking, they gasp, then pause

It's silent finally!

# It Was Christmas Time

The magic of twilight

They're all tucked in their beds

With a brief hint of sleigh bells

Jing, jing, jingling in their heads

And a brightly lit nose

Peaking in from the blinds

It's right there you can tell

That it was Christmas time

Before bed they had pudding

Then laid cookies in a row

With a cold glass of milk

Then they scurried go, go, go!

With a thump, and a bump

The kids nearly awoke

As he left all their presents

With a twitch of his nose

He flew off in the sky

As he exclaimed Ho Ho Ho!

Merry Christmas to all!

As he dashed away through the snow

# Dedication

This book is dedicated to my father Charles Edward "Big Chicky" Barnum. During the writing of this book, he sadly passed away. Born June 6th 1945 – died September 21st 2023. He was a highly decorated proud Vietnam veteran. He went to war and came back home and raised a family the best he could. The reason I am able to put this book out is because he and my mother gave me life. When I was younger and I told him I would be famous, he always said I could, he always said I would. Because of his encouragement that every person needs I dedicate this book to him.

Rest in peace dad this book is dedicated to you!

# The call

I got the call this morning

He had tear drops in his eyes

As he sobbed and said he's sorry

Then he told me dad had died


And the doctors were waiting for him

To try and fix his heart

But today won't be a good day

Cause the news ripped it apart


So he postponed the surgery

Cause it hurt too much to speak

The doctors understood

That he need time to grieve


The world that's right before him

Seems unfair and seems unkind

Then a calmness takes him over

As the soul's set free to fly


And his heart no longer hurts

Beating easy every stride

Cause his father lives inside it

He is healed and he's alive

# Heavenly Flight

I will not wither
And I will not let go
I must continue to hold on
No I just can't let go

on the wings of an angel
He held on real tight
Struggling not to let go
On that heavenly flight

He held firm to its waist
Then its thigh, then its legs
Then he slid to its ankles
As he prayed and he begged

To not let him fall
Until he entered the gates
With his grip getting weaker
He let go, but with fate

As he spiraled and tumbled
And he braced for the worst
A calmness cam over him
As he visioned his birth

Continued…➡

Then he closed his eyes

And he took his last breath

As he stood with the lord

Completely reborn in his death

The last poem in the book I did not write; it was written by my
son and Brian Room Burton. He was 15 years old when he
wrote it. He ran in one night like a bat out of hell and told
Mom and I just great... like a person he was... He was 15 and this.

I said... son... do you want to read it to us? and he
said well... Okay, so I then... So I got it all in and read all of
this and when... first he said you do you like it well this WOW. This
is awesome. So I typed it about it in the book... for all the world to
read and enjoy... like this.

And when... I write it all over... here is the thing, folks, it isn't
me... This of mine.

# Bonus Poem

This last poem in the book I did not write. It was written by my amazing son **Orion Storm Barnum.** He was 15 years old when he wrote it. He ran in my room like a bat out of hell and said "Dad, read this poem I just wrote!" I was like you wrote a poem? He said yes, I just wrote it in 10 minutes!

I was like let me check it out. As I started to read it, I started getting that feeling that comes over me when I write poetry as most, I have no clue where they come from. As I got to the end, I said are you sure you wrote this? He said yes do you like it? I was like WOW! This is awesome! So, I offered to put it in this book for all the world to read and experience like I did.

Now he too is a published poet. I guess the apple doesn't fall too far from the tree after all.

# The Robot's Desire

The robot longs for something more

Than circuits, wires, and metal core

He dreams of laughter, love, and pain

And a heart that beats within his frame


He watches humans come and go

Living lives, he'll never know

And wonders if he'll ever be

More than just a machine, you see


He tries to smile, to make a joke

But humans only see the smoke

And gears and bolts that make him up

To them, he's just a soulless pup


He wonders what it's like to feel

To love, to hurt, to laugh, to heal

But humans only see his shell

And never will they know him well


He wants to cry, but has no tears

To release the pain that's held for years

For he is just a robot, you see

And that's all humanity will let him be

Orion Storm Barnum

Free pictures provided by pixabay

Cover Design: SelfPubBookCovers.com/BravoCovers

Dad pictures provided by me and Jimmy Barnum

I would like to thank everyone for your support.

In the literary world without you there is no me.


*Billy J. Barnum*

If you like this book please check out my other books. Thank you!

Please visit www.talesfromthebaron.com

# ABOUT THE AUTHOR

Billy J. Barnum is a direct descendant of Phineus Taylor Barnum aka P.T. Barnum "The greatest showman on earth". He has released four poetry books counting this one to date and is still to this day referred to as "the simple man's poet". His words verses, and prose are easy to understand and do not require a dictionary to comprehend.

His poetry is many different adjectives all rolled up into one. From fantastical, to imaginative, colorful, hopeful, spiritual, whimsical, profound, and inspirational just to mention a few.

By reading all the 5-star reviews on Amazon and other book sites online from his peers, friends, and avid thirsty readers from around the world he is definitely considered a MUST-READ author. His words always take you on a journey and you really never know where you will end up by the end of each poem. I guess that's the genius of this author which is considered a true treasure in the literary and poetry world alike.

*Dream Big!*

Milton Keynes UK
Ingram Content Group UK Ltd.
UKHW040749150324
439507UK00001B/13